ANIMAL SAFARI

Lemurs

by Kari Schuetz

BELLWETHER MEDIA • MINNEAPOLIS, MN

Note to Librarians, Teachers, and Parents:

Blastoff! Readers are carefully developed by literacy experts and combine standards-based content with developmentally appropriate text.

Level 1 provides the most support through repetition of high-frequency words, light text, predictable sentence patterns, and strong visual support.

Level 2 offers early readers a bit more challenge through varied simple sentences, increased text load, and less repetition of high-frequency words.

Level 3 advances early-fluent readers toward fluency through increased text and concept load, less reliance on visuals, longer sentences, and more literary language.

Level 4 builds reading stamina by providing more text per page, increased use of punctuation, greater variation in sentence patterns, and increasingly challenging vocabulary.

Level 5 encourages children to move from "learning to read" to "reading to learn" by providing even more text, varied writing styles, and less familiar topics.

Whichever book is right for your reader, Blastoff! Readers are the perfect books to build confidence and encourage a love of reading that will last a lifetime!

This edition first published in 2013 by Bellwether Media, Inc.

No part of this publication may be reproduced in whole or in part without written permission of the publisher. For information regarding permission, write to Bellwether Media, Inc., Attention: Permissions Department, 5357 Penn Avenue South, Minneapolis, MN 55419.

Library of Congress Cataloging-in-Publication Data
Schuetz, Kari.
 Lemurs / by Kari Schuetz.
   p. cm. – (Blastoff! readers: animal safari)
 Audience: 4-8.
 Audience: K to grade 3.
 Summary: "Developed by literacy experts for students in kindergarten through grade three, this book introduces lemurs to young readers through leveled text and related photos"– Provided by publisher.
 Includes bibliographical references and index.
 ISBN 978-1-60014-865-1 (hardcover : alk. paper)
 1. Lemurs–Juvenile literature. I. Title.
 QL737.P95S38 2013
 599.8'3–dc23   2012031231

Printed in the United States of America, North Mankato, MN.

Contents

What Are Lemurs?

Lemurs are **primates**. They are related to monkeys and apes.

Some lemurs move on all four legs. Others hop around on their back legs.

Lemurs live on the **island** of Madagascar. Forests and **rain forests** are their homes.

Lemurs eat fruits and plants. Some eat **insects** and other small animals.

Troops

Groups of lemurs are called **troops**. Females rule troops.

Lemurs in a troop **bask** in the sun together.

They also **groom** one another. Their front teeth are like combs.

Lemurs can make themselves smelly. They use their stink to mark their **territory**.

Males also use their stink to fight. They wave their smelly tails at one another!

Glossary

bask—to soak up the warmth of the sun

groom—to clean

insects—small animals with six legs and hard outer bodies; an insect's body is divided into three parts.

island—an area of land surrounded by water

primates—animals that can hold on to things with both their hands and feet

rain forests—warm forests that receive a lot of rain

territory—the land where an animal makes its home

troops—groups of lemurs that live together

To Learn More

AT THE LIBRARY

Buckingham, Suzanne. *Meet the Ring-Tailed Lemur*. New York, N.Y.: Rosen Pub. Group's PowerKids Press, 2009.

Dennard, Deborah. *Lemur Landing: A Story of a Madagascan Tropical Dry Forest*. Norwalk, Conn.: Soundprints, 2001.

Ganeri, Anita. *Lemur*. Chicago, Ill.: Heinemann Library, 2011.

ON THE WEB

Learning more about lemurs is as easy as 1, 2, 3.

1. Go to www.factsurfer.com.

2. Enter "lemurs" into the search box.

3. Click the "Surf" button and you will see a list of related Web sites.

With factsurfer.com, finding more information is just a click away.

Index

The images in this book are reproduced through the courtesy of: Martin Harvey/Getty Images, front cover; Minden Pictures/ SuperStock, pp. 5, 13; Tier und Naturfotografie/SuperStock, p. 7; Visuals Unlimited, Inc./Andres Morya/Getty Images, p. 9; Juan Martinez, p. 11 (large & left); Alexander Chaikin, p. 11 (right); John D. Gorman, p. 15; Tom Uhlman/Alamy, p. 17; Anup Shah/ Animals Animals, p. 19; D & M Sheldon/Age Fotostock, p. 21.